© FLWER PETAL PRESS

To check out our designs
on t-shirts, mugs & more, visit:
HundredthMonkeyTees.com

Happy Birthday to:

On This Day of:

Name:

Birthday Message:

Contact Info:

Name:

Birthday Message:

Contact Info:

Name:

Birthday Message:

Contact Info:

Name:

Birthday Message:

- - - - - - - - - - - - - - - -

- - - - - - - - - - - - - - - -

- - - - - - - - - - - - - - - -

- - - - - - - - - - - - - - - -

Contact Info:

Name:

Birthday Message:

- -

- -

- -

- -

Contact Info:

Name:

Birthday Message:

Contact Info:

Name:

Birthday Message:

Contact Info:

Name:

_____

_____

Birthday Message:

- -

- -

- -

- -

Contact Info:

Name:

- -

- -

Birthday Message:

- -

- -

- -

- -

Contact Info:

Name:

Birthday Message:

Contact Info:

Name:

Birthday Message:

Contact Info:

Name:

Birthday Message:

Contact Info:

Name:

Birthday Message:

Contact Info:

Name:

Birthday Message:

Contact Info:

Name:

Birthday Message:

Contact Info:

Name:

Birthday Message:

Contact Info:

Name:

Birthday Message:

Contact Info:

Name:

Birthday Message:

Contact Info:

Name:

Birthday Message:

Contact Info:

Name:

Birthday Message:

Contact Info:

Name:

Birthday Message:

Contact Info:

Name:

Birthday Message:

Contact Info:

Name:

_____

_____

Birthday Message:

_____

_____

_____

_____

Contact Info:

Name:

Birthday Message:

Contact Info:

Name:

Birthday Message:

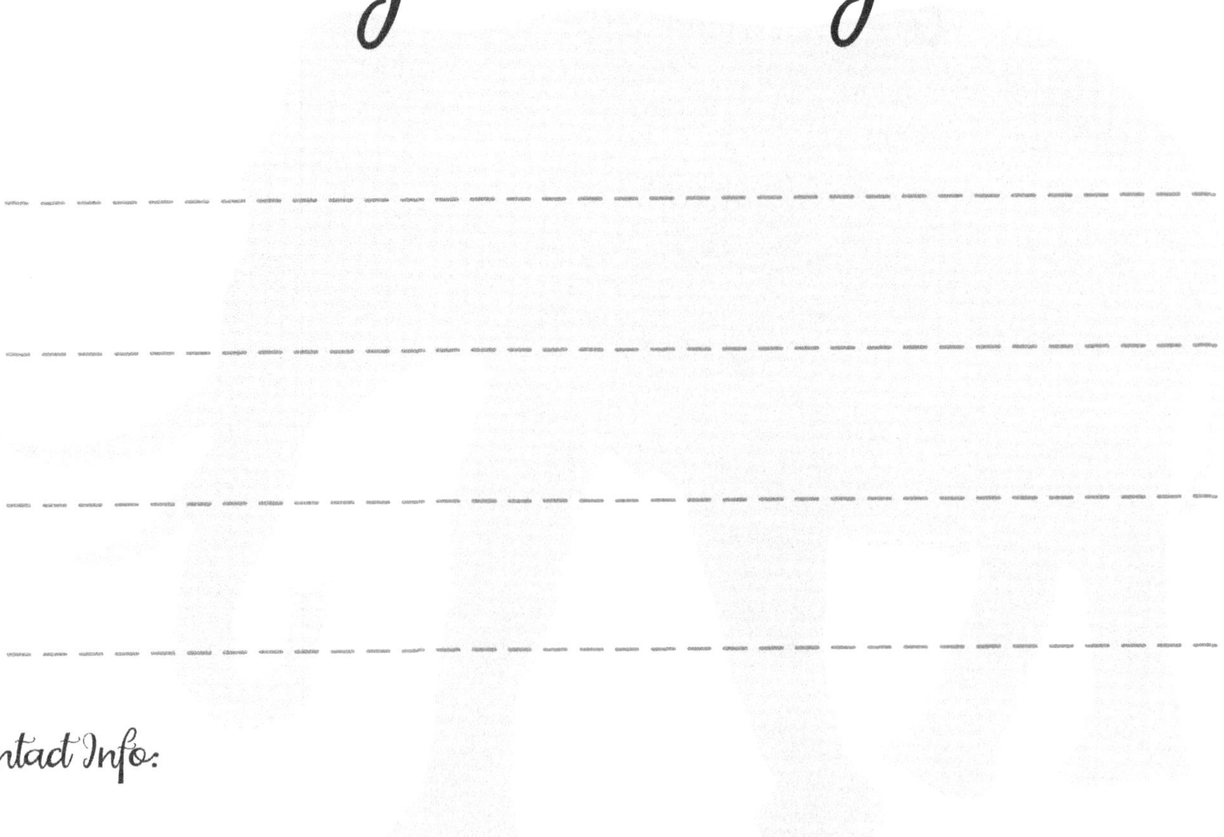

Contact Info:

Name:

Birthday Message:

Contact Info:

Name:

Birthday Message:

Contact Info:

Name:

- -

- -

Birthday Message:

- -

- -

- -

Contact Info:

Name:

_____

_____

Birthday Message:

_____

_____

_____

_____

Contact Info:

Name:

Birthday Message:

Contact Info:

Name:

- -

- -

Birthday Message:

- -

- -

- -

- -

Contact Info:

Name:

Birthday Message:

Contact Info:

Name:

Birthday Message:

Contact Info:

Name:

Birthday Message:

Contact Info:

Name:

Birthday Message:

Contact Info:

Name:

Birthday Message:

Contact Info:

Name:

Birthday Message:

Contact Info:

Name:

Birthday Message:

Contact Info:

Name:

Birthday Message:

Contact Info:

Name:

Birthday Message:

Contact Info:

Name:

Birthday Message:

Contact Info:

Name:

Birthday Message:

Contact Info:

Name:

Birthday Message:

Contact Info:

Name:

Birthday Message:

Contact Info:

Name:

Birthday Message:

Contact Info:

Name:

Birthday Message:

Contact Info:

Name:

- -

- -

Birthday Message:

- -

- -

- -

- -

Contact Info:

Name:

Birthday Message:

Contact Info:

Name:

- -

- -

Birthday Message:

- -

- -

- -

- -

Contact Info:

Name:

Birthday Message:

Contact Info:

Name:

Birthday Message:

Contact Info:

Name:

Birthday Message:

Contact Info:

Name:

Birthday Message:

Contact Info:

Name:

Birthday Message:

Contact Info:

Name:

Birthday Message:

Contact Info:

Name:

Birthday Message:

Contact Info:

Name:

Birthday Message:

Contact Info:

Name:

Birthday Message:

Contact Info:

Name:

Birthday Message:

Contact Info:

Name:

- -

- -

Birthday Message:

- -

- -

- -

- -

Contact Info:

Name:

Birthday Message:

Contact Info:

Name:

Birthday Message:

Contact Info:

Name:

_____

_____

Birthday Message:

_____

_____

_____

_____

Contact Info:

Name:

Birthday Message:

Contact Info:

Name:

Birthday Message:

Contact Info:

Name:

Birthday Message:

Contact Info:

Name:

Birthday Message:

- - - - - - - - - - - - - - - - - - - -

- - - - - - - - - - - - - - - - - - - -

- - - - - - - - - - - - - - - - - - - -

- - - - - - - - - - - - - - - - - - - -

Contact Info:

Name:

Birthday Message:

Contact Info:

Name:

Birthday Message:

Contact Info:

Name:

Birthday Message:

Contact Info:

Name:

Birthday Message:

Contact Info:

Name:

Birthday Message:

Contact Info:

Name:

Birthday Message:

Contact Info:

Name:

Birthday Message:

Contact Info:

Name:

Birthday Message:

- -

- -

- -

- -

Contact Info:

Name:

- -

- -

Birthday Message:

- -

- -

- -

- -

Contact Info:

Name:

Birthday Message:

Contact Info:

Name:

Birthday Message:

Contact Info:

Name:

Birthday Message:

Contact Info:

Name:

Birthday Message:

Contact Info:

Name:

- -

- -

Birthday Message:

- -

- -

- -

- -

Contact Info:

Name:

Birthday Message:

Contact Info:

Name:

Birthday Message:

Contact Info:

Name:

Birthday Message:

Contact Info:

Name:

Birthday Message:

Contact Info:

Name:

Birthday Message:

Contact Info:

Name:

Birthday Message:

Contact Info:

Name:

Birthday Message:

Contact Info:

Name:

Birthday Message:

Contact Info:

Name:

Birthday Message:

Contact Info:

Name:

Birthday Message:

Contact Info:

Name:

_____

_____

Birthday Message:

_____

_____

_____

_____

Contact Info:

Name:

Birthday Message:

Contact Info:

Name:

Birthday Message:

Contact Info:

Name:

- -

- -

Birthday Message:

- -

- -

- -

- -

Contact Info:

Name:

- -

- -

Birthday Message:

- -

- -

- -

Contact Info:

Name:

Birthday Message:

Contact Info:

Name:

Birthday Message:

Contact Info:

Name:

Birthday Message:

Contact Info:

Name:

Birthday Message:

Contact Info:

Gift Log:

Gift Log:

Gift Log:

Gift Log:

Gift Log:

Gift Log:

Made in the USA
Coppell, TX
18 July 2023

19328446R00069